GOD'S MIGHTY HAND

Written by Samuel Durant
Illustrated by Jason Ramasami

Gods Mighty Hand

First published in the UK in 2014

British Library Cataloguing in Publication Data

A record for this book is available from the British Library

ISBN: 9781910587034

Designed by Diane Warnes

Printed in the UK

RESCUING THE ISRAELITES FROM EGYPT

10 Publishing
a division of 10 of those.com

In the land of Canaan,
many many years ago,
A famine struck the region so
that food just would not grow.

The sons of Israel spoke and said,
"This isn't going well!"
So off they went to Egypt,
and in Egypt they did dwell.

After years in Egypt,
that whole generation died,
But just as God had promised them,
Israel had multiplied!

The living God had made them
fruitful by His mighty hand:
They had so many children;
they began to fill the land.

Along came a new King
who had not known of Israel's sons.
He started to get worried
as he looked at all his sums:

"The Hebrews are
too many -
they might beat
us in a war!

Let's make them slaves
and work them hard
so they give birth no more."

They forced them to build cities
and they gave them little food.
They whipped them and they worked them hard
- so cruel and mean and rude!

But Pharaoh's plan backfired
and the land was filled with dread;
The more they were oppressed,
the more the Hebrews grew and spread!

"Right!" said Pharaoh angrily.
"Now I've had enough!
It's time for drastic measures,
time to show them Mr Tough!"
An evil thing he then decreed,
a message mean and vile,

"Take every Hebrew baby boy...
and throw them in the Nile!"

A certain Hebrew couple
had a bouncing baby boy.
They hid him for three months
until they needed a new ploy.

His mother made a basket
(and she made sure it would float).
In river-reeds, with babe inside,
she hid the baby-boat!

While Miriam (the baby's sis)
watched from her hiding place,
She saw someone approaching
and she tried to see their face...
It was Pharaoh's daughter
by the Nile with maids in tow!
"What's that?" asked Pharaoh's daughter,
pointing at Miriam's bro.

She waded in,
reached down and
drew the baby
from the water.

Miriam jumped up and bravely
spoke to Pharaoh's daughter:

"Shall I fetch a Hebrew mum
to nurse this little boy?"

"Yes please! And when
he's older, I will raise
him - what a joy!"

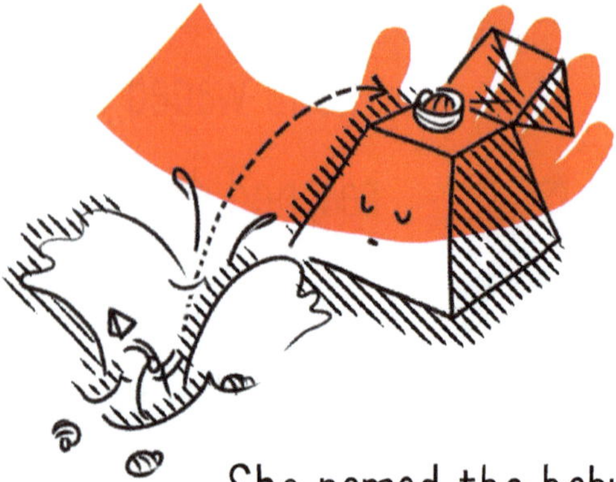

She named the baby Moses
for she drew him from the water
And he grew up in the Palace
with Egyptian Pharaoh's daughter.
He knew he was a Hebrew
and when older he grew sad
On seeing all his kinsfolk
being treated really bad.

One day he saw a Hebrew whipped;
he just could not stand still.
He ran to the Egyptian
and, enraged, he made a kill.

He'd murdered the Egyptian;
took that life with his own hand!
He feared being found out
and hid the body in the sand.

Later, Moses saw two Hebrews
having a dispute,
One said to him:
"You're not my judge!
You murderer! You brute!"

"I've been found out!" thought Moses
and immediately he fled.
He ran away to Midian
and cared for sheep instead.

For many years he lived away
in that far, foreign land.
And meanwhile Israel groaned,
oppressed beneath the
Pharaoh's hand.

They cried out to their God,

"LORD, save us from this misery!"

He heard their cry and acted as

you shall begin to see...

One day, while in the desert,
Moses shepherded his flock:
He led them to Mount Horeb
and then sat down to take stock.
While there he saw a dazzling sight
– a bush with flames of fire.
The flames did not burn up the bush,
so Moses did inquire.

The LORD called from the bush
and, "Moses! Moses!" came the sound.
"You must remove your sandals:
where you stand is holy ground.

I am the God of Abraham
and of his future race."
But Moses feared to look at God
and so he hid his face.

"I've seen My people suffering;
their cry to Me I've heard.
I'll rescue them from slavery
in Egypt - that's My word.
I'll draw them out and place them
in a beautiful green land.
I'm sending you to do this, Moses,
by My mighty hand."

"But who am I to do all this?"
said Moses, feeling small.
"Don't worry, I'll be with you!"
said the mighty Lord of all.
"What are You called?" asked Moses,
"since I do not know Your name.
The Hebrews will all want to know
who sent me back again."

The LORD said, "I am who I am.
Not made; I am pure life.
Tell them, 'I AM has sent me here
to rescue you from strife.'

"What if they don't believe me
when I tell them all of this?"
"I'll help you perform wonders
so they know I'm in their midst."

But Moses was still scared;
he said, "Since I was very young,
I've been no good in public
for I'm slow of speech and tongue!"
The LORD replied, "Who made the
mouth but I? I and no other.
But, even so, to help you
I'll send Aaron too, your brother."

So Moses went to Egypt,
yes he travelled back that way
And told the Hebrews everything
the LORD told him to say.

They heard the news and worshipped,
giving praise to God Most High:
"The LORD has come to rescue us!
The LORD has heard our cry!"

The next day Moses and Aaron
strode off to see Pharaoh.
"The LORD God has commanded you
to let His people go!"
"Who is this 'LORD?'" scoffed Pharaoh.
"No, I will not let them leave.
These Hebrews are just lazy
so more work they will receive!"

Oh dear! They went and told the people
all of this bad news.
"You've made things worse!"
the Hebrews said,
"For Pharaoh did refuse!
And now we have more work to do!"
So Moses went and prayed:

"Oh LORD, why did You send me here?
What is this mess You've made?"

"My plan is still unfolding, Moses,"
was the LORD's reply.
"Now you and all the world will know
I am the LORD Most High.

With mighty wonders I will take
My people from this land;
I'll overthrow their enemies
and save them by My hand."

The people didn't listen
to what Moses had to say.
For they were too discouraged
from their slavery that day!
But Moses and his brother
went back into Pharaoh's court.
"Now let God's people go!" they cried.
"Now free them as you ought!"

But Pharaoh's heart was hardened
by the LORD and he said, "No!"

And so the LORD told Moses,
"To the Nile now you must go."

Then Aaron stretched his staff
over the Nile; that great long flood.
And when he did, the water
of the land turned into blood!

But Pharaoh's heart became more hard:

his answer still the same.

So God called all the frogs

out from the water: out they came!

The frogs were in their bedrooms
and the frogs were in their beds.
The frogs were in their ovens
and the frogs were on their heads!

"Ask the LORD to take the frogs away!"
King Pharaoh cried.
So Moses prayed and all the frogs
upon the land then died.

The people took the dead frogs
and they swept them up in piles.
A horrid thing to see
and you could smell the stench for miles!

Relief then came and Pharaoh made
his heart more hard again,
So God brought forth a plague
of gnats on animals and men.
These gnats made from the dust
attacked the land in such a horde;
The King's magicians said,
"It is the finger of the LORD!"

But Pharaoh wouldn't listen,
no; his heart still like a stone.
So, God sent flies to Egypt
(though they left Hebrews alone).

The flies came in a swarm
which ruined each and every thing.
So, "Off you go," said Pharaoh,
"go and worship God, your King."

The flies were sent away,
but Pharaoh went back on his word.
So God plagued all the livestock:
all the cattle, every herd!
All livestock found in Egypt died
and rotted to the bone.
But not the Hebrew livestock;
all of theirs were left alone.

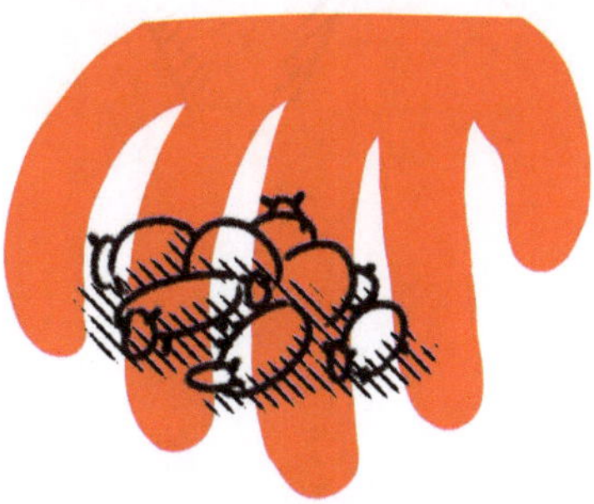

King Pharaoh did not yield,
but he persisted in his sin,
So God caused boils to break out
upon everybody's skin.

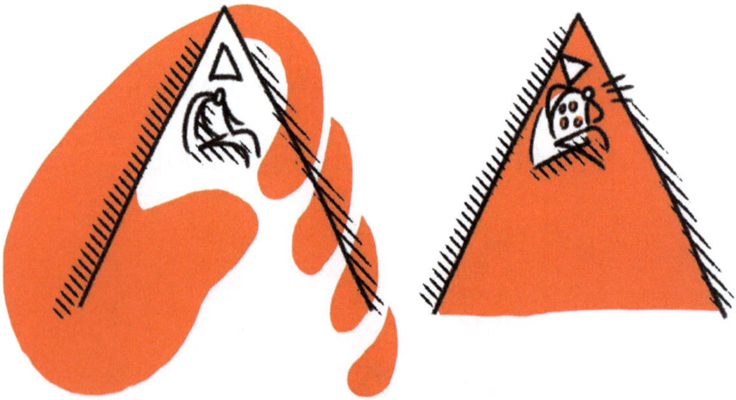

Such itching and such scratching
and such horrid, painful sores:
The King's magicians got them too
and chose to stay indoors!

Despite all this the Pharaoh
set his heart against the LORD.

So God sent down a hailstorm
as had not been seen before.
It killed all those it fell on
and it stripped each tree in sight.
So Pharaoh cried to Moses,
"Stop! Enough! The LORD is right!"

No sooner had it stopped than
Pharaoh turned away again.
So God sent many locusts
which ate all remaining grain.

They swarmed in people's houses -
even in the palace too.
So Pharaoh said to Moses,
"Pray!" He did and they withdrew.

Again God hardened Pharaoh's heart:
he wouldn't set them free.
The LORD sent darkness on the land
so nobody could see!
For three days people groped about
and stumbled round in fear.
Egyptian sun-god 'Ra' was nothing -
that had been made clear.

Then Pharaoh cried out,
"Moses! Do not come in here again!"

So God directed Moses on
the last plague, number ten.

"Now, after this plague Pharaoh
will decide to let you go,
(With presents from Egyptians,
for they fear you now, you know!)."

At midnight I will visit
every household one by one.
And in each household I will then
kill every firstborn son.
But as for Hebrews, have them
paint lamb's blood upon their door:

These houses I'll pass-over and
not touch, you can be sure."

And that is just what happened
on that first Passover night.
The firstborn sons of Egypt were
struck down - a dreadful plight.
The firstborn son of Pharaoh
to the prisoner's eldest boy.
Wailing echoed round the land
- a dark night with no joy.

God's people had believed in Him
and none of them were dead.
They'd followed His commands
and killed a spotless lamb instead.

That very night
the King, dismayed,
cried, "Hurry!
Leave! Just go!"

The Israelites
got ready,
with Egyptian
gifts in tow.

The LORD had said, "Be ready.
Make your bread without its yeast.
And when you go you'll worship Me
and celebrate with a feast!"

Six hundred thousand men along
with each one's family
(As well as some Egyptian friends)
got ready then to flee.

So Moses led this multitude
right up to the Red Sea.
But, looking back, there chasing
them was Pharaoh's great army!

"Ah! Moses! What have you done now?"
the Hebrew people cried.
"You should have left us there in Egypt
- there we should have died!"

But Moses held his staff out
and a mighty wind then hit.
The LORD blew on the water
and the waves began to split.

The waves drew back to form
two walls; a path upon the floor:
The LORD then drew the people out
(like Moses years before)!

The Hebrews all got through -
the water crashed back down again
And swept up the whole army;
all the chariots and men.

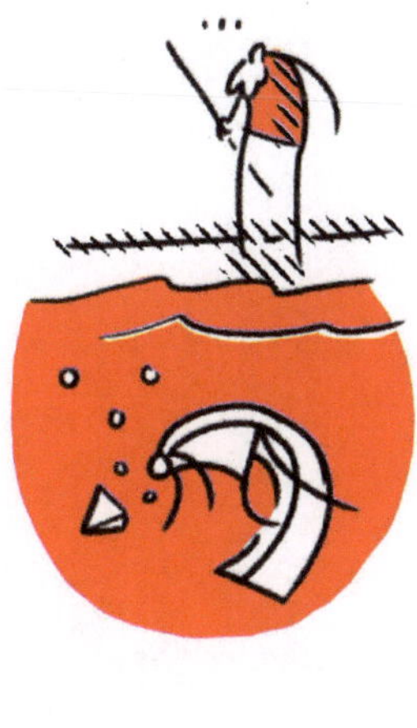

So God defeated Egypt
and He set His people free,
Free to journey on with Him
- no more in slavery!

What an epic story
filled with drama, death and life.
A story of God's work
in saving Israel from their strife.
This same God is at work today -
this same God cares for you.
He keeps on working wonders
for He wants to save you too!

He came and lived as Jesus,
the long-awaited King
And He died just like the lamb
to free us from the chains of sin.

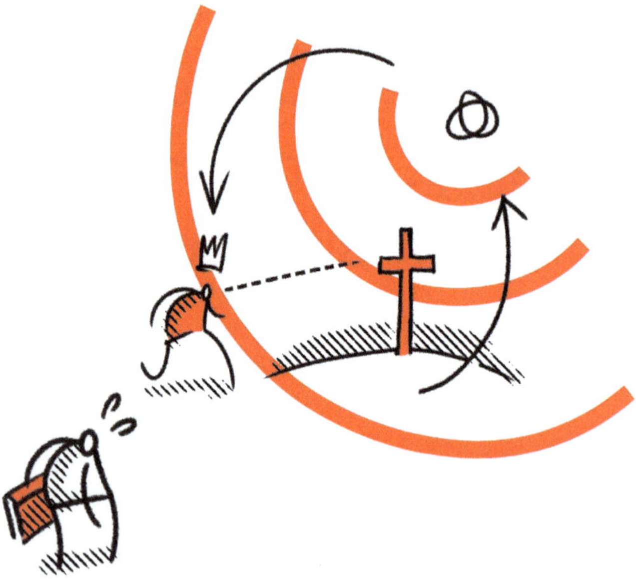

He rose to life again
so we could share His risen power
And He fills us with His Spirit,
working in us hour by hour.

Jesus is alive today
and knocks upon your door:
"Welcome Me into your heart
and live forevermore."

He will never leave you,
even if you're in a mess.
Give your heart to Jesus -
hear His call and answer "Yes!"

If you would like to read more about this story then you can find it in the Bible in the book of Exodus chapters 1 to 14.

10 Publishing
a division of 10 of those.com

10Publishing is the publishing house of **10ofThose**.
It is committed to producing quality Christian resources that are biblical and accessible.

www.10ofthose.com is our online retail arm selling thousands of quality books at discounted prices.

For information contact: **sales@10ofthose.com**
or check out our website: **www.10ofthose.com**